WISDOM

WISDOM

EDITED BY
BENJAMIN UNSETH

GARBORG'S Inc.
Bloomington, MN 55431

Wisdom, The Little Books of Virtue, Series One

Edited by Benjamin Unseth

Copyright © 1995 by Garborg's, Inc.
P. O. Box 20132, Bloomington, MN 55420

ISBN 1-881830-20-9

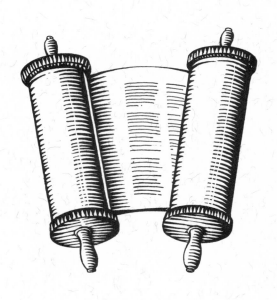

The mark of wisdom is to read aright

the present, and to march with the occasion.

HOMER

To finish the moment, to find the journey's

end in every step of the road, to live the

greatest number of good hours, is wisdom.

RALPH WALDO EMERSON

WISDOM

He who knows not and knows not that

   he knows not,

   He is a fool—shun him;

He who knows not and knows he knows not,

   he is simple—teach him;

He who knows and knows not he knows,

   He is asleep—wake him;

He who knows and knows he knows,

   He is wise—follow him.

ARABIAN PROVERB

WISDOM IS THE SUPREME
PART OF HAPPINESS.

B ut where can wisdom be found? Where does understanding dwell? Man does not comprehend its worth; it cannot be found in the land of the living. The deep says, "It is not in me"; the sea says, "It is not with me." It cannot be bought with the finest gold, nor can its price be weighed in silver....

Where then does wisdom come from? Where does understanding dwell? It is hidden from the eyes of every living thing, concealed even from the birds of the air.... God understands the way to it and he

alone knows where it dwells, for he views the
ends of the earth and sees everything under the
heavens. When he established the force of the
wind and measured out the waters, when he
made a decree for the rain and a path for the
thunderstorm, then he looked at wisdom and
appraised it; he confirmed it and tested it. And
he said to man, "The fear of the Lord—that is
wisdom, and to shun evil is understanding." ❈

JOB 28:12-15, 20-28 NIV

Resolved, never to do anything
which I should be afraid to do if it
were the last hour of my life.

JONATHAN EDWARDS

Wisdom first teaches what is right.

JUVENAL

There is a wisdom of the head, and…a wisdom
of the heart.

CHARLES DICKENS

To know
That which before us lies in daily life
Is the prime wisdom.

JOHN MILTON

The only wisdom we can hope to acquire
Is the wisdom of humility: humility is endless.

GEORGE ELIOT

AESOP

The Boy and the Nuts

A LITTLE BOY once found a jar of nuts on the table.

"I would like some of these nuts," he thought. "I'm sure Mother would give them to me if she were here. I'll take a big handful." So he reached into the jar and grabbed as many as he could hold.

But when he tried to pull his hand out, he found the neck of the jar was too small. His hand was held fast, but he did not want to drop any of the nuts.

He tried again and again, but he couldn't get the whole handful out. At last he began to cry.

Just then his mother came into the room. "What's the matter?" she asked.

"I can't take this handful of nuts out of the jar," sobbed the boy.

"Well, don't be so greedy," his mother replied. "Just take two or three, and you'll have no trouble getting your hand out."

"How easy that was," said the boy as he left the table. "I might have thought of that myself." ❖

The wise want love; and those who love

want wisdom.

PERCY BYSSHE SHELLEY

Reason is a light that God has kindled

in the soul.

ARISTOTLE

Education is not the filling of a pail

but the lighting of a fire.

WILLIAM BUTLER YEATS

THE HIGHEST WISDOM
IS KINDNESS.

THE TALMUD

For God in his wisdom saw to it that the world
would never find God through human brilliance,
and then he stepped in and saved all those who
believed his message, which the world calls foolish.

1 CORINTHIANS 1:21 TLB

Adversity is the first path to truth.

LORD BIGHORN

We are ensnared by the wisdom of the serpent; we are set free by the foolishness of God.

ST. AUGUSTINE

Forewarned, forearmed; to be prepared is half the victory.

MIGUEL DE CERVANTES SAAVEDRA

The wisdom that comes from heaven is first of all pure; then peace loving, considerate, submissive, full of mercy and good fruit, impartial and sincere. Peacemakers who sow in peace raise a harvest of righteousness.

JAMES 3:17,18 NIV

The next best thing to being
wise oneself is to live in a circle
of those who are.

C. S. LEWIS

Wisdom is only found in truth.

GOETHE

WISDOM

e very careful, then, how you live—

not as unwise but as wise, making the

most of every opportunity, because

the days are evil.

EPHESIANS 5:15,16 NIV

WISDOM

16

WISDOM IS KNOWING
WHAT TO DO NEXT;
VIRTUE IS DOING IT.

DAVID STARR JORDAN

A wise old owl sat on an oak,

The more he saw the less he spoke;

The less he spoke the more he heard;

Why aren't we like that wise old bird?

EDWARD HERSEY RICHARDS
A Wise Old Owl

AESOP

The Flies and the Honey Pot

A jar of honey chanced to spill
Its contents on the windowsill
In many a viscous pool and rill.

The flies, attracted by the sweet,
Began so greedily to eat,
They smeared their fragile wings and feet.

With many a twitch and pull in vain
They gasped to get away again,
And died in aromatic pain.

Moral
O foolish creatures that destroy
Themselves for transitory joy.

The proverbs of Solomon son of David, king of Israel: for attaining wisdom and discipline; for understanding words of insight; for acquiring a disciplined and prudent life, doing what is right and just and fair; for giving prudence to the simple, knowledge and discretion to the young—let the wise listen and add to their learning, and let the discerning get guidance—for understanding proverbs and parables, the sayings and riddles of the wise. The fear of the Lord is the beginning of knowledge, but fools despise wisdom and discipline.

PROVERBS 1:1-7 NIV

A man and his wife had the good fortune to

possess a goose that laid a golden egg every day.

Lucky though they were, they soon began to think

they were not getting rich fast enough, and

imagining the bird must be made of gold inside,

they decided to kill it in order to secure the whole

store of precious metal at once. But when they cut

it open they found it was just like any other goose.

Thus, they neither got rich all at once, as they

had hoped, nor enjoyed any longer the daily

addition to their wealth.

A E S O P

The Goose That Laid the Golden Eggs

Time is but the stream I go a-fishing in.
I drink at it; but while I drink I see the sandy
bottom and detect how shallow it is. Its thin
current slides away, but eternity remains.

HENRY DAVID THOREAU
Why I Went to the Woods

Make haste slowly.

BENJAMIN FRANKLIN

What you do when you don't have
to, determines what you will be when
you can no longer help it.

RUDYARD KIPLING

"Think."

SLOGAN OF THE IBM CORPORATION

Instruct a wise man and he will be wiser still;

teach a righteous man and he will add to his

learning.

The fear of the Lord is the beginning of wisdom,

and knowledge of the Holy One is

understanding.

For through me your days will be many,

and years will be added to your life.

If you are wise, your wisdom will reward you. ✤

PROVERBS 9:9-12 NIV

A little nonsense now and then is
relished by the best of men.

The heart is wiser than the intellect.

J. G. HOLLAND

The art of being wise is the art of
knowing what to overlook.

WILLIAM JAMES

IT IS BETTER TO BE WISE AND NOT SEEM SO, THAN TO SEEM WISE AND NOT BE SO.

PLATO

Parents can only give good advice or put children
on the right paths, but the final forming of a
person's character lies in their own hands.

ANNE FRANK
Diary of a Young Girl

God alone knows the depth and the riches of
His Godhead, and Divine wisdom alone can
declare His secrets.

ST. THOMAS AQUINAS

If any of you lacks wisdom, he should ask God,
who gives generously to all without finding fault,
and it will be given to him.

JAMES 1:5 NIV

You cannot make yourself feel

something you do not feel, but you

can make yourself do right in spite

of your feelings.

PEARL S. BUCK

Learn from the mistakes of others,

for you don't have enough time to

make them all yourself!

1 KINGS 3:3-14 NIV

Solomon showed his love for the Lord by walking according to the statutes of his father David, except that he offered sacrifices and burned incense on the high places....

At Gibeon the Lord appeared to Solomon during the night in a dream, and God said, "Ask for whatever you want me to give you."

Solomon answered, "You have shown great kindness to your servant, my father David, because he was faithful to you and righteous and upright in heart. You have continued this great kindness to him and have given him a son to sit on his throne this very day.

"Now, O Lord my God, you have made your servant king in place of my father David.... Your servant is here among the people you have chosen, a great people, too numerous to count or number. So give your servant a discerning heart to govern your people and to distinguish between right and wrong. For who is able to govern this great people of yours?"

The Lord was pleased that Solomon had asked for this. So God said to him, "Since you have asked for this and not for long life or wealth for yourself, nor have asked for the death of your enemies but for discernment in administering justice, I will

do what you have asked. I will give you a
wise and discerning heart, so that there will
never have been anyone like you, nor will
there ever be. Moreover, I will give you what
you have not asked for—both riches and
honor—so that in your lifetime you will
have no equal among kings. And if you
walk in my ways and obey my statutes and
commands as David your father did, I will
give you a long life." ❁

Take time to deliberate, but when

the time for action has arrived, stop

thinking and go in.

NAPOLEON BONAPARTE

God grant me the serenity to

accept the things I cannot change,

courage to change the things I can,

and wisdom to know the difference.

A WISE MAN WILL MAKE
MORE OPPORTUNITIES
THAN HE FINDS.

F R A N C I S   B A C O N

When the issue is not clearly right
or wrong, ask yourself what is wise.

NEVA COYLE

We are weaving the future
on the loom of today.

GRACE DAWSON

WILFERD PETERSON
Slow Me Down, Lord

Slow me down, Lord!

    Ease the pounding of my heart

By the quieting of my mind.

    Steady my harried pace

With a vision of the eternal reach of time.

    Give me,

Amidst the confusions of my day,

The calmness of the everlasting hills.

    Break the tensions of my nerves

With the soothing music of the sighing streams

That live in my memory.

Slow

Help me to know

The magical restoring power of sleep.

Teach me the art

Of taking minute vacations;

Of slowing down to look at a flower;

To chat with an old friend or to make a new one;

To pat a stray dog;

To watch a spider build a web;

To smile at a child;

Or to read a few lines from a good book.

me

down,

Lord!

Remind me each day

That the race is not always to the swift;

That there is more to life than increasing its speed.

Let me look upward

Into the branches of the towering oak

And know that it grew slowly and well.

Slow me down, Lord,

And inspire me to send my roots deep

Into the soil of life's enduring values

That I may grow toward the stars

Of my greater destiny. ❀

It is always wise to stop wishing for things long enough to enjoy the fragrance of those now flowering.

PATRICE GIFFORD

Wise sayings often fall on barren ground; but a kind word is never thrown away.

SIR ARTHUR HELPS

WHATEVER YOU ARE, BE A GOOD ONE.

ABRAHAM LINCOLN

ECCLESIASTES 3:1-8 NIV

There is a time for everything, and a season for

every activity under heaven:

a time to be born and a time to die,

a time to plant and a time to uproot,

a time to kill and a time to heal,

a time to tear down and a time to build,

a time to weep and a time to laugh,

a time to mourn and a time to dance,

a time to scatter stones and a time to

gather them,

a time to embrace and a time to refrain,

a time to search and a time to give up,

a time to keep and a time to throw away,

a time to tear and a time to mend,

a time to be silent and a time to speak,

a time to love and a time to hate,

a time for war and a time for peace. ✿

The heart of a fool is in his mouth, but the mouth of a wise man is in his heart.

BENJAMIN FRANKLIN

We don't get to know anything but what we love.

GOETHE

Abundance of knowledge does not teach men to be wise.

HERACLITUS

KINDNESS IS MORE
IMPORTANT THAN
WISDOM, AND THE
RECOGNITION OF THIS
IS THE BEGINNING
OF WISDOM.

THEODORE ISAAC RUBIN

It is not best to swap horses while
crossing the river.

ABRAHAM LINCOLN
following his nomination to a second term as U. S. President

Wisdom is oft times nearer when we
stoop than when we soar.

WILLIAM WORDSWORTH

It is not wise to be wiser than
is necessary.

PHILIPPE QUINAULT

I know we grow more lovely
   Growing wise.

ALICE CORBIN

One cannot have wisdom without
   living life.

DOROTHY McCALL

Tell her that the lesson taught her
   Far outweighs the pain.

ADELAIDE PROCTOR

Wisdom alone is true ambition's aim,

Wisdom the source of virtue, and of fame,

Obtained with labor, for mankind employed,

And then, when most you share it, best enjoyed.

WILLIAM WHITEHEAD

When I was a boy of 14, my father was so ignorant I could hardly stand to have the old man around. But when I got to be 21, I was astonished at how much the old man had learned in seven years.

MARK TWAIN

That which seems the height of absurdity in one generation often becomes the height of wisdom in the next.

JOHN STUART MILL

Pain makes man think.
Thought makes man wise.
Wisdom makes life endurable.

JOHN PATRICK

Ask counsel of both times—of the ancient time what is best, and of the latter time what is fittest.

FRANCIS BACON

Wisdom too often never comes, and so one ought not to reject it merely because it comes late.

FELIX FRANKFURTER

Our wisdom is no less at the mercy
of fortune than our goods.

LA ROCHEFOUCAULD

The wise does at once what
the fool does at last.

BALTASAR GRACIÁN

MAN STAYS WISE AS
LONG AS HE SEARCHES
FOR WISDOM; AS SOON
AS HE THINKS HE HAS
FOUND IT, HE BECOMES
A FOOL.

THE TALMUD

O H, THE JOYS of those who do not follow evil men's advice, who do not hang around with sinners, scoffing at the things of God: But they delight in doing everything God wants them to, and day and night are always meditating on his laws and thinking about ways to follow him more closely.

They are like trees along a river bank bearing luscious fruit each season without fail. Their leaves shall never wither, and all they do shall prosper.

But for sinners, what a different story! They blow away like chaff before the wind. They are not safe on Judgment Day; they shall not stand among the godly.

For the Lord watches over all the plans and paths of godly men, but the paths of the godless lead to doom.

PSALM 1 TLB

In a moment of insight you can perceive

everything; but it takes years of exactitude

to give it expression.

JOSEPH JOUBERT

Let your old age be childlike, and your

childhood like old age; that is, so that

neither may your wisdom be with pride,

nor your humility without wisdom.

ST. AUGUSTINE

Moral virtues come from habit.... These virtues we acquire by first exercising them, as in the case of other arts. Whatever we learn to do, we learn by actually doing it.... In the same way, by doing just acts we come to be just; by doing self-controlled acts, we come to be self-controlled.... Therefore we must give a certain character to our activities.... In short, the habits we form from childhood make no small difference, but rather they make all the difference. ✿

ARISTOTLE

A prudent question is
one-half of wisdom.

FRANCIS BACON

Wisdom is the ability to use
knowledge so as to meet successfully
the emergencies of life. Men may
acquire knowledge, but wisdom is a
direct gift from God.

BOB JONES

Efficiency is doing something right;
effectiveness comes from doing the
right things.

MAX DePREE

There is often wisdom under a
shabby cloak.

LATIN PROVERB

WISDOM

61

Knowing is not enough; we must apply.

Willing is not enough; we must do.

GOETHE

Knowledge is proud that he has

learned so much; wisdom is humble that he

knows no more.

WILLIAM COWPER

NEVER BE ASHAMED TO
OWN YOU HAVE BEEN IN
THE WRONG, 'TIS BUT
SAYING YOU ARE WISER
TODAY THAN YOU
WERE YESTERDAY.

JONATHAN SWIFT

othing is perfect except your words. Oh, how I love them. I think about them all day long. They make me wiser than my enemies, because they are my constant guide. Yes, wiser than my teachers, for I am ever thinking of your rules. They make me even wiser than the aged.

I have refused to walk the paths of evil for I will remain obedient to your Word. No, I haven't turned away from what you taught me; your words are sweeter than honey.

PSALM 119:96-104 TLB

Knowledge is folly except grace guide it.

ENGLISH PROVERB

There is one thing in the world really worth pursuing—the knowledge of God.

ROBERT H. BENSON

WISDOM

65

Wisdom and virtue are like the
two wheels of a cart.

JAPANESE PROVERB

The true sage is not he who sees, but
he who, seeing the furthest, has the
deepest love for mankind.

MAURICE MAETERLINCK

THE ROAD TO WISDOM?—
WELL, IT'S PLAIN AND SIMPLE
TO EXPRESS:
ERR AND ERR AND ERR AGAIN
BUT LESS AND LESS AND LESS.

PIET HEIN
The Road to Wisdom

A wise man will not leave the right to the mercy of chance, nor wish it to prevail through the power of the majority. There is but little virtue in the action of masses of men.

HENRY DAVID THOREAU

There are no secrets of success. Success is doing the thing you know you should do. Success is not doing the things you know you should not do. Success is discovering your best talents, skills, and abilities, and applying them where they will make the most effective contribution to your fellow man. Success is not arriving at the summit of a mountain as a final destination. It is a continuing upward spiral of progress. It is perpetual growth. ✿

WILFERD PETERSON
The Art of Living

Nine-tenths of wisdom is being wise in time.

THEODORE ROOSEVELT

Buy the truth and do not sell it;

get wisdom, discipline and understanding.

PROVERBS 23:23 NIV

Judgment is not upon all occasions

required, but discretion is.

LORD CHESTERFIELD

I earnestly desire you may have wisdom—that from all the flowers of learning you may draw the honey and leave the rest.

BRILLIANA HARLEY
Letter to her son

He that can have patience, can have what he will.

BENJAMIN FRANKLIN

ane had fallen into the error that many people do, of thinking *age* is *experience;* that passing through a certain number of those events that crowd round our path, is experience; whereas, it is not born of time, but of thought, of investigation. Like all other treasures of the mind, we find it within. The fountain of wisdom lies deep in our own hearts, and it is there we must seek for it. ❖

HANNAH FARNHAM LEE

WISDOM

ONLY A FOOL TESTS THE DEPTH OF THE WATER WITH BOTH FEET.

AFRICAN PROVERB

Those who would know much, and love little, will ever remain at but the beginning of a godly life.

METCHILD VON MAGDEBURG

Wisdom never kicks at the iron walls it can't bring down.

OLIVE SCHREINER

What parent can tell when some fragmentary gift of knowledge or wisdom will enrich her children's lives? Or how a small seed of information passed from one generation to another may generate a new science, a new industry—a seed which neither the giver nor the receiver can truly evaluate at the time.

HELENA RUBINSTEIN

Government is a contrivance of human wisdom
to provide for human wants. Men have a right that
these wants should be provided for by this wisdom.

EDMUND BURKE

We should be careful to get out of an experience
only the wisdom that is in it—and stop there; lest
we be like the cat that sits down on a hot stove lid.
She will never sit down on a hot stove lid again—
and that is well; but also she will never sit down on
a cold one any more.

MARK TWAIN

KNOWLEDGE COMES, BUT WISDOM LINGERS.

ALFRED, LORD TENNYSON

A wise reserve seasons the aims and
matures the means.

BALTASAR

T o know how to grow old is the masterwork
of wisdom, and one of the most difficult
chapters in the great art of living.

HENRI FRÉDÉRIC AMIEL

God made the earth by his power; he founded the world by his wisdom and stretched out the heavens by his understanding. When he thunders, the waters in the heavens roar; he makes clouds rise from the ends of the earth. He sends lightning with the rain and brings out the wind from his storehouses.

JEREMIAH 10:12,13 NIV

WISDOM

79

SAMUEL WADSWORTH LONGFELLOW
Go Forth to Life

Go forth to life, oh! child of Earth.

Still mindful of thy heavenly birth;

Thou art not here for ease or sin,

But manhood's noble crown to win.

Though passion's fires are in thy soul,

Thy spirit can their flames control;

Though tempters strong beset thy way,

Thy spirit is more strong than they.

Go on from innocence of youth

To manly pureness, manly truth;

God's angels still are near to save,

And God himself doth help the brave.

Then forth to life, oh! child of Earth,

Be worthy of thy heavenly birth,

For noble service thou art here;

Thy brothers help, thy God revere! ❧

O World, thou choosest not the better part!

It is not wisdom to be only wise,

And on the inward vision close the eyes,

But it is wisdom to believe the heart.

Columbus found a world, and had no chart,

Save one that faith deciphered in the skies;

To trust the soul's invincible surmise

Was all his science and his only art. ❀

GEORGE SANTAYANA

HE WHO HAS BEGUN
HAS HALF DONE.
DARE TO BE WISE;
BEGIN!

QUINTUS HORATIUS FLACCUS

Two frogs lived together in a marsh. But one hot summer the marsh dried up, and they left it to look for another place to live in, for frogs like damp places if they can get them. By and by they came to a deep well, and one of them looked down into it, and said to the other, "This looks a nice cool place. Let us jump in and settle here." But the other, who had a wiser head on his shoulders, replied, "Not so fast, my friend.

Supposing this well dried up like the marsh, how

should we get out again?"

Think twice before you act.

AESOP
The Frogs and the Well

ECCLESIASTES 11:7-10; 12:1,13,14 TLB

It is a wonderful thing to be alive! If a person lives to be very old, let him rejoice in every day of life, but let him also remember that eternity is far longer, and that everything down here is futile in comparison.

Young man, it's wonderful to be young! Enjoy every minute of it! Do all you want to; take in everything, but realize that you must account to God for everything you do. So banish grief and pain, but remember that youth, with a whole life before it, can make serious mistakes.

Don't let the excitement of being young cause you to forget about your Creator....

Here is my final conclusion: fear God and obey his commandments, for this is the entire duty of man. For God will judge us for everything we do, including every hidden thing, good or bad.

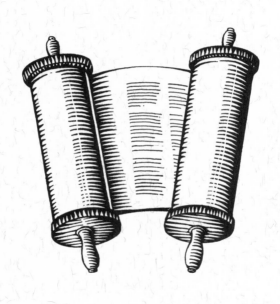